A Practical Guide to Mental Hygiene

by Charu

I dedicate this book to Dr. Jonn Mumford, one of my amazing teachers who recently transitioned to the other side. He empowered me as a teacher with wisdom, patience, and humility.

D1714722

Charisma was understood as a gift or talent divinely bestowed. Highly likable, warm-hearted, consummate communicator, naturally empathetic... Mix those with Belizean cool and you've got Charu. Most charismatic souls get overwhelmed by their gifts. They forget the source and purpose of those blessings. In the early 90's Charu embraced his calling. He understood. "I'm meant for helping others": body, mind, and spirit.

A Practical Guide to Mental Hygiene is the natural fruit of Charu's 30 years of dedicated study, practice, and teaching. He presents in clear terms the lofty concepts from the Vedic wisdom tradition. The essence: We are spiritual beings enmeshed in a material body made up of senses, mind, intelligence, and false ego. We are burdened, troubled by our involvement with matter. While yearning for freedom and pure love, we tend to fall prey to the pushings of our lower nature.

Decades of guiding and mentoring mixed with innate talent works wonders. Charu has been a devout student of prominent teachers in a variety of disciplines. He has imbibed, digested, and refined the art of presenting. As I was reading A Practical Guide to Mental Hygiene, a mantra emerged: "I can relate to that ". The perennial yoga classic, Bhagavad Gita, speaks of the senses as "so strong and impetuous that they forcibly carry away the mind even of a person of discrimination endeavoring to control them." Yep, I can relate to that. And of the mind being the "friend or enemy of the embodied soul." My mind as my enemy... I can certainly relate to that. And of the false ego which covers the self; wildly delusional and shameless. But senses, mind, and the ego are all gifts. Used in goodness, they elevate and liberate us and others. But one must learn the art...

A Practical Guide to Mental Hygiene is practical. The end of each chapter gives a simple, effective technique for directing and tempering each of these powerful components of our embodied life.

Modern life can be hectic, often overwhelming. "No time" seems like a reality. But sparing some quota for developing our self is essential. This is a guide book to be regularly referred to for clarifying our vision of life and realigning our bearings.

Charu has been elevating his students for decades. Now he makes a valuable offering to reach a broader audience. I'm proud of his work and grateful to have him as a true friend on the path.

--Tara Das, Director of Bohemian Tours

First and foremost, I would like to thank my wife, Yvonne Borree, for inspiring me to practice the teachings that are within these pages. I am also grateful for Ann Spence who encouraged me to write the book. I am grateful to Caroline Cowen for final editing. My artist friend Nikunja Vilasisni's art work has captured my imagination, for that I am ever grateful. Susan Hu, thank you for proofreading and to Samiyyah Andrewin for the layout and all that you did to help manifest this humble project. Without you all, the book would still be in my mind. So thank you, thank you, thank you.

Table Of Contents

How to Use this Book   **1**

1 l A Universe of Dualities   **4**

Mental Hygiene Technique for
Mental Health   **10**

2 l Modes of Material Nature   **15**

Mental Hygiene Technique on
the Three Modes of Nature   **23**

3 l The Mind and Time   **26**

Mental Hygiene Technique on
Time   **34**

**4 l The Mind and the Sense of
Sight**   **39**

Mental Hygiene Technique for
the Sense of Sight   **49**

**5 l The Mind and the Sense of
Hearing**   **53**

Mental Hygiene Technique for
the Sense of Hearing   **65**

6 l The Mind and the Sense of Taste   **69**

Mental Hygiene Technique for the Sense of Taste   **79**

7 l The Mind and the Sense of Smell   **83**

Mental Hygiene Technique for the Sense of Smell   **91**

8 l The Mind and the Sense of Touch   **95**

Mental Hygiene Technique for the Sense of Touch   **103**

9 l The Mind and the Intellect   **108**

Mental Hygiene Technique on the Mind and Intellect   **119**

10 l Living in the Present Moment, A Present from God   **124**

Mental Hygiene Technique for Living in the Present   **134**

How to Use this Book

This book has been written with the intention that the reader will understand the theory and put the theory into practice through the techniques. At the end of each chapter, there is a Mental Hygiene practice. It is recommended to read the theory first, then do the practice that follows. You may want to read all the theory first, then go back to the practices, and that is absolutely fine. Reread the Mental Hygiene practices a few times before doing them. This will allow you to gracefully practice them step by step, as recommended.

Each practice takes between 8 and 15 minutes. We spend roughly the same time for our daily dental hygiene. Both the mind and the teeth are important. But we also know that the mind is more important. Hence, let us practice our Mental Hygiene daily as well.

Every day in our lives, a different sense may be pulling us away from our Mental Balance. It is recommended to reread the chapter that corresponds to the specific sense, and perform the corresponding practice that day. Maybe one day, one of the modes of nature is overriding you, reread chapter 2. One day, if you just want to contemplate on time, reread chapter 3, etc.

Once you become familiar with the practices, you may choose to do them alone. Over a period of time, you will notice how the practices make you calmer and more peaceful in your everyday life. Read, Relax, and Enjoy.

DUALITIES OF
THE MIND & THE UNIVERSE

1 I A Universe of Dualities

As spiritual beings who are experiencing life through the body and mind, we all want to be good and do good. We have a desire to live in a peaceful society, which respects every living entity as a fellow spiritual brother and sister. We want to inspire each other to be the best forms of ourselves. With the deep profound love in our hearts we want to serve and protect the old, the young, the sick, and the healthy. Yet, when we open our eyes and ears on any given day, it is easy for us to see and hear the news and realize that we are living in challenging times. There is a lot of good and beauty around us, but also a lot of unnecessary destruction, exploitation, and disturbed human beings. We may even question our own mental stability, our own mental sanity.

One thing we can all agree on is that life is a very complex experience, and that human beings are complex organisms as well, similar to plants and animals.

When we see the physical body of a fellow human being made up of the skin, nails, hair, etc., we can understand it is very complex. Within this complexity, we are living in a universe of duality. One duality is having a physical body made up of earth water, fire, air, and ether, while we also have a subtle body made up of the mind, intellect, and ego which is invisible to the human eye.

We may communicate with each other through the physical body by touch and sight, but not with the mind and intellect. We must wait for someone to speak before we get a glimpse of how evolved their intellect is, and what type of emotions are running through their minds.

Since our human form (micro universe) is a subset of the vast macro universe, it is subjected to duality as well. If we cut the body down the center we will find a right side and a left side of the body. An eye, ear, arm, leg, and brain on either side.

This is so, because all the elements of the body are borrowed from the universe. The air in the lungs comes from the outer universe. Similarly, the heat in the body comes from the sun outside. Same as the water, which comes from the ocean. Hence, we can recognize that duality first starts with the outer universe – the sun and the moon. The magnetic pull for these celestial bodies affects our bodies and minds. They govern our day and night. We rise when the sun rises, and we become active beings; we go to sleep with the moon to rejuvenate and restore our minds and bodies. Our body gets energy from the sun, while our minds get energy from the moon hence; our mental state fluctuates like the moon. As the moon wanes and waxes, our mental state changes too. Sometimes, a person can be calm and balanced, and a minute later, they are chaotic with their words and actions.

This duality is very very complex, and as we evolve every day, we see examples in the body and mind.

Politicians are powerful people. Most of the time, they are voted in by locals, so they can increase the betterment of life, providing education, health, jobs, food, and military protection. But what makes a politician stand by their words after being elected, in selfless service for the citizens, while, on the other hand, we find politicians who say one thing when they're campaigning about serving society and then when they're elected they do the opposite, and serve themselves. The politicians and possibly their own families achieve betterment of life, while other citizens are stuck, and sometimes experience life getting even worse.

The media is a powerful tool. Media influences the thinking of the masses. What pushes some media outlets to tell the truth, even when it might have a backlash on their funding, while another media continuously reports fabricated news to serve a private agenda?

The next two are close to home. I'm a yoga teacher, and you can find yoga teachers who are responsible, care for their students, empower them to evolve in their practice gradually without forcing them into postures where their bodies will ache. These teachers respect a student's boundaries and adjust out of compassion. Then, there are yoga teachers who teach out of false ego. These teachers attempt to establish themselves as the best yoga teachers, subjugating their students as if they are less than them, and even adjusting them with passion which can start to manifest sexual exploitation.

We find spiritual teachers who practice what they teach: the ancient texts. We may find them manifesting qualities of knowledge of the spiritual self, humility, compassion and service for all beings, no matter race, bloodline, or religion.

Then, we find those who teach incomplete realizations. They teach a separatist dogma instead of a philosophy of seeing everyone as a child of God. They teach "isms" that separate us from other living entities. They teach religions that divide us. We are encouraged to find fault with other religions, trying to establish that other religions are less than others. Eventually missing the point that we are all brothers, sisters, and children of God.

We can go on and on with these dualities. What is good to know is that, in this universe, everything is transient. It only lasts for a while. If we find ourselves in one of the dualities, as above mentioned, it is not permanent. If we find ourselves in the positive frequency of the duality, know that we can fall into the negative frequency. By negative association of people and environment, we can change. We might find ourselves in one of the above negative mental states, but if we achieve the positive association of people and environment, we can also change to a positive frequency. Let's embrace these dualities and learn from them, use them as stepping stones to our Mental Clarity and Peaceful Heart.

Mental Hygiene Technique for Mental Health

Come into a nice comfortable seated posture, whether it's sitting in a chair or on the floor, cross-legged. Keep the spine tall. The palms can be on the lap or the palms can be on the knees, tip of the thumbs touching the tip of the index fingers. Close the eyes softly and bring the whole body into stillness. (1 min)

Bring the mind into the present moment, witnessing the breath at the entrance of the nostrils. Be aware of the breath moving in and out of the nose. (1 min)

Now, gaze into the center of the eyebrows, as you gaze there, imagine a beautiful sunrise you have witnessed. As the sun rises, see it rising up, up, up. It's directly overhead, midday. Now see the sun starts to go down. See the sun setting. (1 min)

As it disappears, now see the moon rise. See the beautiful full moon coming out of the ocean, next it's overhead. Then the moon travels over the sky. The moon starts to set. (1 min)

Imagine you can see the sun rising and the moon setting. You can see both in the sky, and you recognize the sun is there. Daytime, it lasts for a while. The moon is there. Nighttime, it lasts for a while. "Everything in the universe only lasts for a While." Sit with this realization. (1 min)

As you understand this duality of the universe. You're going to have ups in life. It will last for a while. You'll have downs. It will last for a while. Now remember one of the minor set-backs you had in life, and remember that it only lasted for a while. (1 min)

Now remember one of the amazing ups you had in life, and remember, also, that it only lasted for a while. (1 min)

As you see the dualities of the universe only last for a while, when you go forward, henceforth in life, you will see dualities in your daily life. Always remember that it only lasts for a while. Today, you will respect the ups, you will respect the downs, and you deal with them, knowing that they are both temporary.

The mind will remain calm and steady. You won't get too happy. You won't get too sad. I will get happy, but I know it will only last for a while. I will get sad, but I know it will only last for a while. With this attitude, you can keep the mind very balanced.

Mentally repeat three times: "Every experience I have in this life with my body and mind are temporary experiences, my mind will remain calm and steady in both experiences."

Bring your awareness back to the breath. Realizing the breath is keeping your body alive, your mind active, your intellect active. Grateful for that which will allow you to put the philosophy of the temporary nature of the world outside. Move forward in the sacred life with higher understanding. It's a transient place, like the sun and the moon.

Take a deep inhalation. Exhale slowly, bring the breath back to normal. Open your eyes to the world outside. With this understanding, I will tolerate experiences, just as I learn from them.

Three
MODES OF
NATURE

14

2 | Modes of Material Nature

This beautiful universe that we're living in is controlled, or one might say governed, by the three modes of nature. Not one centimeter of this universe can escape the three modes. They are the mode of goodness, passion, and ignorance. These three modes have distinct qualities by which they can be identified, and they are always competing for dominance over the spiritual being who has taken a material body.

The mode of goodness can be identified as cleanliness. Someone might have a clean body, clean home, clean office, and wear clean clothes. This mode can also be identified in moderation. Someone eats in moderation, sleeps in moderation, works in moderation, has intercourse in moderation, recreates in moderation. The mode of goodness is characterized by a sense of happiness that comes from other people being involved. Other people's happiness gives you happiness. Knowledge that raises the vibration to know that I am a spiritual being. This is the mode of goodness.

The mode of passion can be identified by desires that drive us out of balance. Take, for example, someone's eating habits. They might be eating too much, which stems from a lot of greed in their minds, never satisfied. They overindulge in work, sex, and just about everything else in their life. They sleep very little. They focus their knowledge on how to get more out of this material world. Their homes are often decorated with art that triggers passion. People governed by this mode love the colors red and orange. This is the mode of passion.

The mode of ignorance can be identified by sleep. You might know someone who sleeps too much. Their consciousness is darker, because knowledge does not reside there. The only expression of knowledge is for the body. This mode is characterized by inertia. A person governed by the mode of ignorance procrastinates, and takes a long time to do anything. When they do something, they may do it foolishly. The clothing they wear is dirty. Their mind resides in madness. This is the mode of ignorance.

These three modes of nature are always competing amongst themselves to influence the living beings in all species of life. They pervade, not just the living entities, but the whole universe, hence the environment as well. If you are in the mode of goodness, you like to be in a pleasant environment where you will find calmness and peacefulness. Maybe you live near the beach, you like the park, a lot of trees, waterfalls. For the mode of passion, the environment requires a lot of action. We find this environment in big cities where there is a lot of movement, cars, and people. The mode of ignorance is very dark. Somewhere like underground railway stations, underground subways, nightclubs. It's dark and loud, without any tranquillity.

Food is another category where we can see and distinguish the modes of nature. Foods in the mode of goodness are fresh. They are healthy. They are not overcooked, and they are not undercooked.

Foods in the mode of passion are spicy foods, chilies, and peppers. These foods raise the level of passion in us. An example of food in the mode of ignorance is canned foods. These foods sit on a shelf for six months to a year, with a lot of preservatives. This type of food doesn't give life to the cells of the organs. Foods in the mode of ignorance deplete the organs.

The company we keep is another example of the three modes. In the mode of goodness you choose to be around someone who gives off goodness or balance, and their company inspires you to come to that mode. If you are around someone who is very passionate, governed by the mode of passion, they may be focused on me, myself, and I, or perhaps too passionate to focus on others. Then we have examples of people in the mode of ignorance. They tend to ignore or cause harm to other living entities. Constantly killing animals, killing humans, destroying their own personalities.

These are just some examples of how the three modes of nature pervade our planet and our material universe. Since our material bodies, in the form of a (fish, bird, human, etc.) are composed of material elements, they are controlled by the three modes. We may have the micro-universe in the form of our physical and subtle bodies. Yes, it's a subset of the macro universe. All the elements that make up our physical and subtle bodies are borrowed from the macro universe.

The physical body that we see is made up of the elements: earth, water, fire, air, and ether. The skin and the bones are made up from the earth and water element. 85% of the physical body is water. That water comes in the form of blood, plasma, cerebral fluid, urine, and saliva. We borrow that water from the ocean. The water you have in your body right now, that you drank in the last hour, for example, came from the ocean outside.

The fire element makes our bodies warm. This fire comes from the sun. The air that we have in our bodies, comes from the air outside. Our bodies have a certain dimension. The height, width and weight, which occupies our space. This space is part of the universal space.

Every species has an individual mind, but that mind is borrowed from the universal mind. This is the place where emotions and thoughts run through. Then we have the intellect. Each and every one of us has a level of intelligence that we also borrow from universal intelligence.

As we can see, the universe outside is intelligent. The sun rises every day and sets every evening, the moon rises and sets nightly. One moment the moon is full, and 15 days later it is a new moon. 15 days later, it's a full moon again. The planets orbiting around the sun with different gravitational pulls is another example of universal intelligence. On our planet we have 4 seasons which follow an intelligent pattern. Winter is followed by spring, spring followed by summer, summer by autumn and again, winter.

Then we also find that a living entity has an ego. The ego that we all have, we borrow from the universal ego. That perception of 'I am something.'

Again, these three modes of nature pervade the entire universe. When a living entity (spiritual being) takes birth in a certain species, let's say we are in the human species, we get a gross body made up of the elements, earth, water, fire, air, ether, and a subtle body made up of mind, intellect, and ego. All these put together are governed by the three modes of nature that constantly influence us. Sometimes in the human mind, we experience the mode of goodness, sometimes the mode of passion, and sometimes the mode of ignorance.

In the early morning, when we get up, we experience the mode of goodness. As the sun comes up, midday, we're moving around the mode of passion. Then, when the sun goes down, and the darkness rises in the night, we go to sleep in darkness. Then ignorance kicks in.

So, we can easily see how the three modes control us and every other living entity. As we evolve, we start to understand how categorizing the three modes helps us to recognize when they're affecting us, and how we, the spiritual being, can start to work toward the mode of goodness or balance. When we achieve the mode of goodness more and more in our daily life, we can use that mode of goodness as a springboard to go into deep spiritual evolution to make the mind our best friend.

As we evolve, we can then respect the mode of ignorance. We know the body needs to sleep. We can respect the mode of passion, because we need to fulfill certain desires in moderation. And we can learn to respect the mode of goodness, which helps us to attain clarity, triggering us to question, who am I? What is this universe about?

Mental Hygiene Technique on the Three Modes of Nature

Come into a nice, comfortable seated posture, whether it's sitting in a chair or on the floor, cross-legged. Keep the spine tall. The palms can be on the lap or the palms can be on the knees, tip of the thumbs touching the tip of the index fingers. Close the eyes softly and bring the whole body into stillness. (1 min)

Bring the mind into the present moment by witnessing the breath at the entrance of the nostrils. Be aware of the breath moving in and out of the nose. (1 min)

Next, gaze into the center of the eyebrows and visualize a rainbow in front of a green-covered mountain and bright, blue sky. (1 min)

Now visualize a busy street from the top of a building at midday. Watch the cars, and people crossing the street. See them moving fast. Hear the noise of horns beeping, bicycle bells ringing, and street vendors calling out their products. (1 min)

Visualize a dark night. People are sleeping, lights turn out, everyone's body is at rest. (1 min)

Lastly, mentally repeat three times: "I am in the mode of Goodness more and more to balance the modes of Passion and Ignorance."

Bring your awareness back to the breath. Take a deep inhalation, exhale slowly. Open the eyelids, and venture out into the world with more goodness in your being.

MIND in the
PAST, PRESENT
and FUTURE

3 | The Mind and Time

Mind and time are two powerful, subtle forces to which we cannot see. When someone looks at you, they will see your physical body, but they won't see your mind. That doesn't mean your mind doesn't exist. We cannot smell, taste, or touch time. That doesn't mean time doesn't exist. As little babies when we were born into this world, we were taught about the elements first. What is water? We learned it is wet. What is fire? We learned it burns. What is earth? We learned it is solid and can walk on it. What is air? It carries aroma and increases our sense of touch. What is space? We learned it is everywhere, and we are within it, and it allows sound waves to travel. After a while, our parents or guardians, our teachers, introduced us to a new word: Time.

As we started to grow, our culture shared words with us and our vocabulary increased. Eventually we learned the words yesterday, tomorrow, and now. Our conversations developed around these words, so our minds began to understand them, even as very young children, but only gradually do we understand more of this force called Time.

If you are able to travel back into your memory, you might remember the first time a family member or your teacher at school introduced you to a beautiful clock. You would remember it had 12 numbers in a circle, with a long hand and a short hand. Then you were taught how to read the clock. We all learned that a clock connects us to a force called Time.

Ancient cultures, among them our ancestors, understood that a clock measures a force that is expressed through the relationship and movement of our planet Earth and that of the sun and moon. Today, like our ancestors, we have the same experience. When the sun comes up, we become energized. This is called the day. When the sun goes down, the world (or our part of it) becomes dark. The stars come out, and we can see the other planets. This is called the night.

Even as a little baby, we began to understand a rhythm between these two powerful forces, these celestial bodies called the sun and the moon, with the clock. We understood, "Oh, it only has 12 numbers; 1 all the way to 12."

Depending on which part of the planet you were born in, most people will see that it is bright for about 12 to 14 hours, and then it is dark for another 10 to 12 hours. On other parts of the planet, which are further away from the equator, this depends on the seasons. In some places, there are 22 hours of brightness, and only 2 hours of darkness. At other times, in a different season, there might be 22 hours of darkness, and 2 hours of brightness. Regardless of where we live and the length of our days, we all began to understand the sun and the moon, and to associate them with day and night. These celestial bodies help us understand the rhythm of time.

As we continued to develop, we grew more in tune with this 24-hour cycle. In the daytime, when the sun is up, we feel energetic, and we want to accomplish lots of things.

As nighttime comes in, and the moon rises, our mind and our body become lethargic, we feel tired, and then we go to sleep. All of us as humans became conditioned in this way. We become accustomed to the experience, and then we know in our minds that it will only be dark for a while before the sun comes up again.

When the sun rises again, we begin to understand, "the experiences that I had when the sun was up the previous day, we call that, Yesterday." In this way, our mind began to also understand what we call the past.

Then, even as little children, we understood this word Tomorrow. We might think, "In this world that I'm living, with today and yesterday, there is Tomorrow. Tomorrow is for the things I can't accomplish today, or whatever I didn't finish. I'll be able to do them when the sun rises again, tomorrow." In this way, the mind began to move from today into the future. Our little minds started to grasp those two words, past and future, with the movement of the sun and the moon from yesterday into tomorrow.

We all eventually recognized the 24-hour sequence. Our guardians might have introduced that sequence of hours as a day. Next, we were introduced to a calendar, which is simply another method to measure time. We were taught that the calendar measures 24-hours in weeks. One week is seven times of the rising of the sun and setting of the sun, the rising of the moon, and setting of the moon. Those seven days become a week. The four weeks we see on a calendar make a month. Then we understood, depending on which part of the planet we were living, that three of those months make a season. Or, if you're closer to the equator, six of those months make a season - one wet and one dry. Then, we understood 365 days of the rising and setting of the sun, rising and setting of the moon, makes a calendar year.

As we understood the phase of the week, the mind learned to project, "Oh, that was in the past, last week." The mind became able to jump the seven-day cycle, thinking about the future or "next week."

We looked at the month in the calendar, and our mind and intellect evolved, "Oh, in the past, last month I did this. I did that." We spoke to our friends and family. Next, the mind projected into the future, and in our conversation we said, "Oh, next month I'm planning to go here or go there."

It expanded from there. Last season we did this. Next season we're going to do this. The mind started to understand, "Oh, after 365 days is last year." As we continued to grow, we saw that we did certain things in certain months. On certain days of the week, we went to school. On certain days, we didn't go to school. Certain months are cold. Certain months are warm. Our mind started to understand the cycle of this subtle, gentle force called time.

Then at some point we realized, "Oh wait, I have no power over this force called time." We understood the force of time is constant. It never stops. It keeps pushing us forward.

Then we started to question, "Wait, wait, how can I go back in time?" Then we realized that we cannot go back in time with the body. Only with the Mind. The physical body is moving forward. It's aging, and will continue to age.

Let's examine this beautiful word, Age. We first learned about it through birthdays. On the day of our birth, we heard this word. The next year it means you are one year, or 365 days, older. The mind and the intellect started to calculate time in our own sweet way. "Okay, in five years," we start to think, "I will be..." Or, "I'm five years old, in five years I'll be 10. In 10 years, I'll be 15." The mind can start to project with the intellect. We understood how time works, and we understood, "Wait, my body cannot go back." When this happened, we learned to appreciate another phase of time called Now.

We came across this word, Now, which denotes a time in the present moment. We rarely connect to the present today, to Now as a moment.

Instead, in our culture, Now is stretched out or elongated over a phase of time. If someone says, "Oh, I'm eating now," our mind conceptualizes it, "Oh, they will be eating in the now for the next 10 to 15 minutes." Or, "I am doing laundry now." Our mind connects now to this activity for 30 to 45 minutes. But if we pay attention and begin to spend time with the now, we can bring the now into the actual present moment. When people of the past practiced mental hygiene by bringing their mind into the present, by looking at the sun or moon, they would connect their vision to the present moment, to anything happening at that moment.

Mentally, they would say, "I am seeing the sun, the moon, this is the present moment. My reality is now." If we do this, we can begin to live in the present moment as our ancestors did.

When I am eating, this is the present. This is my reality. This is my now. When I'm walking through the park, this is my reality. Whatever I'm seeing. This is my now. We can then start to bring that now more and more into a smaller phase of time where we can bring it to the exact second, exact moment. If the mind can be in that exact moment more and more regularly, the past and future sleep. The mind becomes peaceful. As our bodies grow older, we see that most of our mind swings like a pendulum in time. We're either living out memories from the past, or we are setting goals for the future. We're grateful that we have been engineered like this, but we want to spend more and more time now, in the present moment. Please open the Present of the present moment, a sacred gift from God.

Mental Hygiene Technique on Time

Bring your body into a nice, comfortable seated posture, either in a chair or on the floor. Cross-legged, the palms can be on the lap, or on your knees. Touch the tip of your index fingers to the tip of your thumbs. Close your eyes softly. Bring the whole body into stillness. (1 min)

Bring the mind into the present moment, bring your awareness to the breath at the entrance of the nostrils. Try not to control the breath, just witness it moving in and out. (1 min)

Bring your focus to the center of the eyebrows, and as you gaze there, know that you are gazing into the present moment. Know that in this life, you can move into the past, into the memory. I want you to move back to the past when you did something positive. (1 min)

Next, I want you to project your mind into the future. You can set goals. I want you to plant a desire in the future, something you're going to do tomorrow. Something that is positive. Mentally repeat it, "tomorrow I will do such and such." (1 min)

Now, bring the mind back into the present moment by gazing into the center of the eyebrows. Try not to think of anything, just witness the space.

If random thoughts come up from the past or future, that is natural; witness them with detachment. A thought may enter the mind, stay for a while, and then leave. The mind will become quiet again. Another thought may come in. It will also leave, and you will find quietness again. Stay in the present moment, in that beautiful quiet space. (2 mins)

Become grateful for the element of time. It is a beautiful force which we work with throughout our lives. We used it in the past. We are using it now. It subtly pushes us into the future. We are working with time. Be grateful for the time force. Know that we have an allotted amount of time on the planet. Think to yourself, with the rest of the time I have on the planet, I want to do something positive for the betterment of my mind and body, for the betterment of the planet, and the betterment of the universe.

Bring the mind back to the breath, at the entrance of the nostrils. The breath keeps you in the present. Spend more and more time in the present moment. Take a deep inhalation. Exhale slowly. Breath back to normal. Open your eyes, and live your amazing life in the present moment more and more.

MIND AND THE SENSE OF SIGHT

4 | The Mind and the Sense of Sight

Each and every one of us is engineered with two amazing, beautiful eyes. The fetus developed in our mother's womb, and at a certain point in time, these two eyes started to develop, complete with the lens, cornea, and retina. The optical nerve connects to the occipital lobe of the brain, so we can develop something we call vision. We use our eyes to connect with forms, and those forms from *outside*, project a form in the mind *inside*. Something else is necessary, however. We are only able to see, because there is light in our world.

As the universe was engineered, the element of fire was created. The primary source of fire in our universe is the sun. There's a beautiful interrelationship between the sun and the eyes.

Could you imagine if God made all of us with beautiful eyes, some green, some blue, some brown, and some gray, and then God forgot to create the sun? What would be the use for our beautiful eyes? We would have eyes, but we wouldn't be able to see.

So, there is an interrelationship with the element fire and our eyes with their sense of sight. For the eyes to perform their function, to see, they depend on the fire element. The fire element (en)lightens our world. We see a form, we get an image of the form from outside, and we bring it into the mind. There is another important aspect in this connection. We were also gifted with the part of our body called eyelids. The eyelids are able to move up and down, and importantly, to close them. The covered frontal part of the eyes allows us to take a break from the rays of the light. When we take a break from the rays of the light, it becomes dark. We are engineered to have time when we can see things, and time to relax our eyes.

It is interesting to note that as we cover the eyes with the eyelids, something else happens. Inner vision starts. Somehow, even without light, we can still see or bring images to the mind. As the mind and eyes develop as a child, the images will be governed by the three modes of nature. In the mode of goodness, we might see a beautiful sunrise. The image enters the mind, and it produces a certain level of happiness. We see a sunset, and the mind becomes peaceful. The first time anyone sees a rainbow, with all the different beautiful colors planting a beautiful image in our mind, they experience a sense of inner peace and happiness. When we see the stars at night, for the first time as we're developing, it triggers the mode of goodness. It triggers questions, *who am I? Why am I on this planet? What is the moon? What is the sun?* We begin to question. When the eyes are connected to the mode of goodness through our vision, we become peaceful and calm, as well as questioning in a way that is peaceful and calm. Every day we open our eyes, and we can allow our mind to either evolve or devolve. If the eyes connect to forms that are in the mode of goodness, our mind evolves.

We continue to develop calmness, peacefulness, and appreciation for beauty. The beauty of this universe, the beauty of God's creation, the beauty in people, the beauty in animals. We see, and we realize, this is a beautiful form.

When the eyes are exposed to forms in the mode of passion, something else may develop within us. We may develop emotions of selfishness, and even exploitation. We want to enjoy a form. We want to experience that form. These experiences are always happening, so even as a child is growing, we're growing the mind too. Exposure to a particular mode cultivates the emotions connected to that mode. Today, in our culture, we are able to see movies. Some of them are very passionate. We see people sharing sex appeal, and the mode of passion pervading their minds. We become attracted to seeing the form of someone unclothed. A person might even become attached to pornography, receiving some short-lived enjoyment.

When the mode of passion covers our intelligence, we experience enjoyment from seeing another living entity exploited. We don't recognize what our eyes are seeing. The people on the screen are just actors, and once the movie is cut, those beautiful souls are suffering in their own minds and bodies, because someone has exploited them.

There is also the mode of ignorance. If the eyes see through the mode of ignorance, we become attracted to seeing forms that lead to self-destruction. As a child grows up, the child sees an adult smoking or taking drugs. "Oh, what's that?" The child might think. "I can try that when I get a little older." Even the earliest visions create a seed in our minds. Before we can understand it, we are manifesting the same habits ourselves. This happens especially when we are going through a challenging phase in our life journey. Even though we know smoke is bad for our lungs and drugs are full of toxins which break down our organs and make us lose mental balance, when the mode of ignorance takes over we may make poor decisions, which in turn make us perform regrettable harmful acts to ourselves and others.

Once the mode of ignorance is in us, we don't want to see movies that are passionate, or sensual. We don't want to see movies that are very beautiful and raise our vibration. We want to see movies that contain self-destruction. We get attached to it. And the more we watch those types of movies, in the genre of horror, for example, the more we want to act those movies in some fashion in our lives. As we evolve, we want to see things that aid in our evolution. God gave us eyes, but we need to learn how to use the eyes in moderation. It's hard to not see forms of self-destruction. Walk on the street you'll see someone smoking, taking drugs, or drinking alcohol to excess.

This is where our own efforts come in. If we want to evolve, we have to raise our vibration. Let's replace forms that we see with the mode of goodness, more, and more. You could think, "If I want to bring peace into my mind, I need to be attracted to forms which uplift me."

In the culture today, along with ignorance and passion, there is goodness. By training our eyes in the mode of goodness, we can help ourselves to evolve. Try to find a way to rise early, and see a sunrise. If that is not possible, then put yourself in a situation where you can see a sunset. Take a break from the computer, and experience nature. See the mountains, see the waterfalls, see the gorges, see the butterflies. See natural beauty, even if it is inside an urban park. It will bring a sense of inner tranquillity that will encourage you to look for the mode of goodness more and more. This will also help trigger the intellectual questions such as who I am, and who created my eyes, the light, and the beautiful forms that I see. You'll start to have a deeper appreciation for the fire element, your eyes, and their relationship.

When we see something, it means that we are having a relationship with that form. As we look to the sun, moon, and stars, a certain relationship develops.

In the mode of goodness, this relationship brings respect for that form. When we watch the sunrise, we may realize that we have a personal relationship with the source of fire, the sun. Our gratitude for the fire element will continue to grow. This doesn't mean we will live a life where we don't look at anything else. Every day we are in situations where we see forms in the mode of goodness, passion, and ignorance. But every day we can refine this.

As we evolve, we want to be able to see beautiful things in the mode of goodness, and then gradually reduce the mode of passion. Gradually also reduce the mode of ignorance. We have free will. We can choose. Each and every one of us has chosen to watch things in the mode of ignorance. Each and every one of us has chosen to watch things in the mode of passion. Each and every one of us has chosen to watch things in the mode of goodness.

When we choose, we know the feedback that goes into the mind and body. The mode of ignorance, self-destruction. The mode of passion, exploitation of another living entity. When we see the mode of goodness, liberation of the consciousness. We begin to respect each other, as well as other living entities.

The eyes are powerful. Respect them, cherish them. Remember also to respect the eyelids, which give us a break from the sun rays. So we can go in and allow our body to go to sleep and recover. Respect the eyelashes which keep the dust particles out of the eyes. Be grateful for how the eyes were created. The more and more we evolve, gratitude kicks in. God's intelligence went into engineering our eyes. We can question how many eyelashes we have, how the eyelids are there to cover. Could you imagine if we didn't have any eyelids? We would walk around with our eyes wide open. We would go to sleep with them wide open. So grateful for the Engineer of the eyes and the sense of sight.

What we see brings calmness, brings creativity, or brings destruction in the mind. What we see influences the mind powerfully. The more we get attracted to those forms, when we go to sleep, our dreams will be influenced by them. If we watch a movie, in the mode of ignorance, destruction, a horror movie, we most likely will have challenging dreams, nightmares. If we watch passionate movies just before going to sleep, we probably will have sexual dreams. If we watch a movie which is uplifting or if we gaze at the stars, the moon, the ocean, they will influence peaceful dreams. So as we know how the modes work through the sense of sight, then every day let's improve a little bit to the mode of goodness more and more and more. Raising the vibration of the mind from self-destruction to self exploration and selfishness to selflessness. Let the eyes raise our vibration to respect others and offer selfless service to them.

Mental Hygiene Technique for the Sense of Sight

Sit in a comfortable chair or cross-legged on the floor. Keep your spine tall. Whatever is comfortable for you. Bring the whole body into stillness. The palms can be on your lap or on your knees. Close your eyes softly. Bring the whole body into stillness. (1 min)

Bring your awareness to the breath at the entrance of the nostrils. Try not to control the breath, just witness it moving in and out. (1 min)

Now move your awareness to that space behind the forehead. The space where the mind is occupying. As you gaze there, imagine your beautiful eyes. You have the eyeballs, grateful for the eyeballs. Grateful for cornea. Grateful for the optic nerve. Grateful for the eyelid. Grateful for the eyelashes. (1 min)

Now imagine something you saw with your eyes in the last 24 hours that was in the mode of goodness. Something very beautiful. Maybe a beautiful being, maybe a mountaintop, a sunrise, a rainbow. (1 min)

Now use the power of your memory to remember something you saw in the last 24 hours or the last week that was in the mode of passion. See people moving around. You see transportation of cars or planes. You see motion, moving, very passionately. (1 min)

Now remember something you saw in the last 24 hours that was very in ignorance. You see another creature harming another creature, causing pain to someone else. (1 min)

Next, imagine you can also see spirituality around you. You can see divinity around you. Transcendental vision. You are able to see a spiritual being, a spark within everyone's heart, in the animal's heart, plant heart, human heart. Recognizing the bodies are only moving because there's a spiritual being there. (1 min)

For the next 24 hours, I want you to plant in your mind "along with the three modes that I will also see the spiritual beings throughout the day, see living beings as their spiritual self." Repeat it mentally three times now. (1 min)

Now bring your awareness back to the breath. Recognizing the eyes will only be active, your mind and intellect will only be active, if the breath is there. Grateful for the breath, which keeps us alive. Take a deep inhalation. Exhale slowly. Bring the breath back to normal breathing. Open the eyelids, ready to meet the sun, its rays and the world with your amazing eyes.

MIND AND THE SENSE OF HEARING

5 I The Mind and the Sense of Hearing

Each and every one of us has been engineered with a beautiful sense of hearing. We have two beautiful ears, comprised of the outer, middle and inner ear, the eardrum, and the auditory nerve, which connects to the auditory cortex at the temporal lobe of the brain. These nerves allow us to register sounds and connect them to our intellect, so we can understand what type of sounds we're hearing. As a little fetus develops in the mother's womb, the ears are also developing. The temporal lobe of the brain is developing. The auditory nerve is developing. Simultaneously, the first material element is developing. We call it space or ether. The fetus will begin to develop within this space, and it is through the medium of space that sound vibration travels. Even as a little fetus, we begin to hear sounds before we can touch, see, taste or smell.

The first sound we heard is the sound of the mother's heartbeat. We became familiar with that sound. Boom, boom, boom. After a baby's birth, we often bring the baby close to the mother's heart. The baby will stop crying because the baby recognizes the sound of the mother's heartbeat. What we call space, or ether, is essential because even as we are gifted with two beautiful ears, if there was no ether or space in the universe, we wouldn't be able to hear one another. Our ears have a special relationship with the space element. If you put someone in a vacuum, (in which there is no space) they would not be able to hear you. Our ears are divinely created. Simultaneously, the space element is divinely created. The more we contemplate the sense of hearing, we become grateful for space, knowing that this is the medium that allows us to hear.

Whichever culture we were born into, whether it's Asian, African, North American, South American, or European culture, as we were developing as little kids we would begin to hear words from that culture.

As our brain, intellect, voice box and ears developed, we were able to hear and respond. We developed an ability for speaking our language.

The whole universe is vibrating and anything that vibrates creates sound. We are able to hear high-pitched sounds, low-pitched sounds and sometimes can't hear other sounds as our human sense of hearing is limited. Scientists have proven that different animals hear frequencies that are higher and lower than what the human ear can hear. Our human species is engineered to be able to comprehend a certain range of sound frequencies.

Sound pervades our culture as we're growing, and these sounds manifest through the three modes of nature. The three modes of nature encapsulates all of our listening. Sometimes we hear sounds in the mode of goodness, sometimes in passion, and other times in ignorance. Sounds in the mode of goodness relax us. These sounds calm us down, and make us peaceful.

For example, the soothing sound of a gentle breeze whistling through the trees. Or when we visit the beach, and the waves gently flow in and out. The sound of the ocean surf is very soothing and relaxing. Another example is gentle rainfall on the roof, the sound is very calm and therapeutic. It relaxes us.

The same sounds channeled through the mode of passion create a feeling of activity in us. These sounds make us want to move. If you go to the same beach and the waves are rough, we won't feel relaxed. We feel the need to move. If it's raining too hard, it becomes very hard to relax because of the loud sound of the rainfall on the roof. So sounds of nature may come in different modes.

The sounds of nature may also come in the mode of ignorance. When the rain comes as a heavy storm and picks up into a hurricane, it's destructive. We hear the rain and it doesn't calm us. It brings fear in us. The heavy lightning and thunder destroy our peace. It's very destructive. We might lose our lives from this kind of storm.

Similarly, we might be on the beach when the waves crash with too much power. This creates fear in us. The sounds of nature can arrive in all three categories.

Similarly, as we start to develop our conversations, we begin to hear words and phrases that fit into the three modes. We hear words that are pleasant, such as when someone greets you. "Have a very good morning," a person might say. When someone recognizes that you're a special person, they might greet you any time of the day and share words of recognition. "You look nice today," or, "You inspire us today." These are words in the mode of goodness. In the mode of passion, we hear conversations that trigger passionate desires. "Hello gorgeous, you're sexy." These words might trigger passion in us. Or we might hear words in the mode of ignorance that are very destructive. If someone says, "I don't like you", "I'm going to harm your family. I'm going to harm you." That sound vibration comes in with harm, and it creates a different energy in us, the mode of ignorance.

As we age, we get introduced to music. Every genre of music on the planet fits into the three categories as well. Whether it's rock, reggae, classical or hip hop music, they all fit into the three modes of nature. Some classical music can be very calm and peaceful, and listening to it, we will feel relaxed. The nervous system becomes soothed. Some classical music is very passionate. It goes very fast. Some classical music is in the mode of ignorance as well. You hear it and it drains you. You may feel depressed after listening to it.

I grew up with reggae music, and you can experience the three modes also with reggae. Some songs such as, "One love, one heart." The lyrics continue, "Let's get together and feel alright." These musical sounds and the accompanying lyrics raise the vibration. We feel that we are one beautiful people, all together on this planet. Next, you might hear the sounds of a different song, with different lyrics, "Hello, girl, hello guy, you look good. I want to connect with you. I want to make love to you." These lyrics are very passionate.

Then again, you might hear a song with lyrics such as "Let's go and spliff. Let's smoke this. Let's get irie." Then, if you follow the instructions, and you smoke too much, you will want to go to sleep feeling lethargic. In every genre of music, you'll find the three modes of nature. As we start to evolve, we realize that some music makes us positive, some makes us feel aggressive, or exploit other living entities, and some music just makes us lethargic. We may begin to understand that sound vibration has a strong control over us.

The sounds in the media are also very important. The media helps structure our thinking. A big part of our mental development occurs through the media. People in the media, in advertising and marketing especially, are experts at what they do. They understand that they can affect the choices we make. They have enormous control over the masses. As we evolve, we understand that we want to make our own choices in life. If someone else makes our choices for us, we will never be happy, but unfortunately, many of the choices we make today are made or guided by other people, especially by our exposure to the media.

The media knows this. They are paid millions of dollars for advertisements or to spread propaganda. We might hear a conversation on the TV about a shirt or a bag, or even a pair of shoes. An awareness of desire develops in our mind. Then, when we step outside and see the same shirt or bag advertised on the bus, or at the bus stop, and before you know it, we're walking into a store to buy this bag or shirt, or whatever it is. The media can affect our actions, guiding our choices. After we buy the product, we're still not happy because it wasn't really our choice.

Then, of course, there are the news channels. News is far from straightforward. A lot of news is biased one way or another. Different channels give us different news, or different interpretations of the news, to control our minds and how we choose to understand. You may find yourself representing a political party or some corporation because of propaganda. One channel rarely gives both sides of the news.

An intelligent person will begin to question, wondering if it is possible to hear from other sources, before coming to a conclusion, and will proceed by doing some deeper research. We can't accept everything at face value that we hear in the media, especially with the news. We have to be very careful. We have to filter it. We have to see what resonates with our higher self.

All of the content producers in TV and moviemakers in Hollywood are amazing at understanding how to provoke and induce emotions to heighten the impact of their work. A movie always has sound effects. Even before movies had sounds (words), music played along to induce different emotions at different places in a film.

After we watch a movie that's in the mode of goodness, we leave the theater feeling inspired. We might want to do good, save and protect the planet, plant trees, or save the dolphins.

Then, some movies make us very passionate. They might induce sensual feelings, making you want to share feelings with another person sexually. The sound vibration and visual experience creates these feelings in us. Next, there are some sounds in the movies that are very destructive, in the mode of ignorance. We hear cars crashing, guns killing people, entire cities destroyed. These sounds stay with us. When we leave the movie, the sounds create a pattern within us. Before we know it, if we're not balanced enough, we may want to engage in destructive activities as well. So, let's choose our movies carefully.

There are also transcendental sounds in this universe. These sounds tap into the spiritual self. If you go to churches and hear the gospel singing, or the choirs, you are hearing people connecting to divinity through their sacred voice and the vibration through the Adam's apple. In the mosque, we hear sacred prayers repeated with devotion to connect to Allah. In the yoga culture, we find yogis and yoginis dedicated to chanting sacred mantras on beads and in group kirtan.

We find Buddhist monks chanting Om and other mantras for purification and healing. In Synagogues, we find Rabbis leading the Jewish community in sacred prayers from the Torah. We hear Cantors dedicated to singing the verses of the Torah. Every one of us, it doesn't matter which spiritual culture we were born into, we will see people engaging in silent prayer, silently speaking to divinity directly. We might also see them using a mala or a rosary or a set of beads, making a sacred number of sounds to connect with divinity, through transcendental sound.

As Sounds enter our minds, the vibrations enter our memory. From time to time, a sound vibration may come up in our mind, from our memory, and before we know it, we're singing a song silently or we're chanting our mantras, and then our body starts to move side to side. Sounds from the mode of ignorance may also come back to us from our memory. Before we know it, we may feel ourselves wanting to do something destructive.

Sometimes when you're feeling peaceful and calm, an inner sound may enter the mind and make us more peaceful. Sometimes from memory, a sound of passion comes in, and we may think we need to move, or accomplish something. You might think, "Let me go do this. Let me go do that. I need to go get this job. I need to go run. I need to exercise."

Sounds are constantly coming up from the subconscious mind, and if we cultivate our mind where we listen to more sounds in the mode of goodness and transcendental sound, it will help us to counter the passionate and the destructive sounds that are all around us.

We can't avoid ignorant sounds. We can't avoid passionate sounds. We can't avoid sounds in the mode of goodness. So, as we start to purify our mind, we want to make our mind our best friend. This means that we begin to choose, out of our free will, sounds which raise our vibration, which brings peace, which allow us to walk around as a vibration in the mode of goodness more and more and more.

We can demonstrate what peace of a mind is: an extension of that sacred sound in the mind. When people hear you, their minds will become peaceful. When people have a conversation with you, their mind and body will become more peaceful and they will feel happier around you.

We are grateful for the temporal lobe of the brain. Grateful for the auditory nerve. Grateful for the element of ether, of space.

Mental Hygiene Technique for the Sense of Hearing

Come into a nice, comfortable seated posture either sitting on a chair, or on the floor, keeping the spine tall. Palms on the lap, or palms on the knees touching the tip of the index fingers to the tip of the thumbs. Close your eyes softly. Bring the whole body into stillness. (1 min)

Bring your mind to the breath at the entrance of the nostrils, feeling the air moving in and out. Just be with the breath. (1 min)

Move your awareness to the right outer ear, then the middle ear, lastly to the inner ear. (1 min)

Move your awareness to the left outer ear, then middle ear, lastly to the inner ear. (1 min)

Move your awareness to the center of the eyebrows. Become grateful for the ears (1 min)

Now imagine, in the last 24 hours, some vibration that you heard that was not pleasant. They were destructive sounds. The words create a vibration within you to harm another creature by exploiting them one way or another. (1 min)

Now remember some sound vibration you heard in the last 24 hours, when you heard it, it allowed you to become very passionate about something. You heard it, and you wanted to do something, move, be creative, something positive. (1 min)

Now I want you to remember sounds in the last 24 hours that were very uplifting. Make you happy, make others around you happy, cheerful. (1 min)

Lastly, I want you to focus on your mind's eye, remember some sacred sounds you've heard. Whether it's prayers, whether it's from gospel sounds, sacred sounds from your spiritual texts. Maybe it's mantras. Remember one of those sacred sounds now. Raise your vibration to connect to higher forces, to divinity. Mentally repeat that sacred sound again and again. (2 mins)

Bring your awareness back to the breath, recognizing the breath brings in fresh air, fresh life force. It keeps the ears and brain active. Become grateful for the breath. Take a deep inhalation, exhale slowly. Open your eyes slowly, and listen to the sounds around you right now, and identify which mode of nature you're hearing at this moment.

MIND and SENSE of TASTE

6 | The Mind and the Sense of Taste

We all love to eat. This is true across the board, except for a few people who are breatharians. Human beings are engineered with the amazing gift of a tongue, connected through the facial and glossopharyngeal nerves to the insular cortex of the brain, allowing us to develop the sense of taste. The taste buds develop through the medium of water. The element of water allows us to taste. If there was no water on the tongue, we wouldn't be able to decipher different tastes. So, water is essential, and we become grateful for the water element.

If God only created our tongue but didn't create water, we wouldn't be able to taste our food. We can understand the interrelationship between the tongue and water.

Depending on which culture we are born into, we develop a certain taste according to the three modes of nature. While our little fetus was developing in our mother's womb, our mother, according to her culture, had a certain attraction to the types of food she ate. The food the mother eats goes into the stomach and affects the fetus. So, we develop similar taste buds to our mother and father.

If, at the time when we're in our mother's womb, our mother eats fresh food, we develop a taste for that. Spicy food, we develop a taste for that. Decomposed food, such as canned food, we will also develop a taste for that. We can see the three modes of nature that control our type of eating. As we take birth, whichever part of the planet we are, we will develop a certain taste through that culture and within the three modes.

If we're in the mode of goodness, we'll eat food that is fresh, juicy, live, or living foods. These foods have a lot of the sun and moon's energy, for example, fruits and vegetables.

If the mode of passion controls our tongue, we'll become attracted to spicy food, such as chilies and peppers. We may also become attracted to food that is violent. In other words, any food which is prepared through violence such as meat products.

If our taste buds are controlled through the mode of ignorance, we will develop an attraction for food that is processed, or food that is in a can. Canned food sits on a shelf for six months, or more, decaying and losing nutrients. Similarly, food that is overcooked is in the mode of ignorance. When food is overcooked, enzymes and nutrients disappear. We develop a taste for these types of food when we are in the mode of ignorance.

We can understand that in each culture around the world, you can see these three modes represented in different types of food. I grew up in the Caribbean, and my culture at the time was part of a developing country.

My great-grandparents used to eat fresh food off the earth in mode of goodness. By the time I grew up, we had shifted because it was cheaper to buy canned food. So, I grew up with a lot of canned food, decomposed food, with a lot of added chemicals added to preserve it. That's food in the mode of ignorance. Then along with that, about 20% of my plate of my food was violent food. I grew up eating meat, passionate food. Maybe 5% of my diet was salad or fresh fruit. On my plate I would see three modes of nature.

Around the world, you can see this happen regularly. Someone sits down to eat, and they'll have food on their plate from three modes: a salad, which is in the mode of goodness, a piece of meat, which is in the mode of passion, and maybe there's something processed, or from a can, right on the same plate. The type of food we eat affects the mind. If we eat too much processed food, we will become very lethargic. We become sleepy, or tired.

If we eat too much passionate food, food that has been violently acquired, that aggressiveness comes into our minds and bodies as well. Our mind will become aggressive to other humans and to other living entities. The mind will seldom find peace. If we eat food in the mode of goodness, fresh fruits, vegetables, non-violent food, our mind becomes peaceful more easily. We can sit in stillness and enter a place of quietness with less effort. This will allow our relationships with other people to become more graceful too.

Since we have free will, most of the time we can choose which mode to eat in. I have friends brought up in the mode of goodness. Their parents were vegetarians. They had never eaten meat up to their adult life. At some point in their adult life, they had a choice to remain vegetarian or to try violent food.

Some of my friends tried eating meat and then realized how it affected their mind and body. They then returned to vegetarianism. I also have some friends who are so content with vegetarian food, they remain vegetarian their whole life.

There are also people like me who grew up on meat and processed food, and using our free will come in contact with the mode of compassion. This is the understanding that a nonviolent diet helps make my mind peaceful. It doesn't matter where we come from, where we were born, or what type of food your taste buds have been engineered to enjoy. At some point, as we evolve, we begin to question, what am I putting in my body that has given me energy, that has given me life?

As we grow, our tongue develops a taste for sweet, sour, salty, bitter, spicy, and pungent tastes. As we evolve, we don't want to overeat. Even if the food is in the mode of goodness, you want to eat in moderation, because you want to keep the organs vibrant.

There is also something known as eating in the mode of transcendence. Around the world, people in different cultures, different religions offer their food to divinity, to God. They recognize the food has been provided by God, and they say a gentle prayer of gratitude, asking the Lord to bless the food. The blessing helps the energy of the food to evolve our consciousness spiritually. In many cultures around the world, people offer their food with love to their deity, to God, and then they take it back. What they eat are the remnants, the leftovers, of God.

Instead of just eating, we honor the food. We become grateful for the tongue and the water element. Gratitude spreads to the chef, to those who planted the seeds, to those who transported the food from the farm to the shop and to the shop owners who organize where we can purchase it. We become grateful eventually for all those who allowed God's grace to come onto the plate. This is a higher way of eating, or eating with the intellect.

When we honor the food, we want to honor it in the mode of goodness. Sometimes honoring it in the mode of goodness means we eat without talking. We eat in silence. This way we can really taste and connect with divinity through the food. Maybe you can try this for one meal once a day, or once a week.

At other times, we might eat in the mode of passion. At these times, we are eating and speaking to other people. The air that was meant to bring the energy into the stomach goes out and our digestion strength weakens. Eating in the mode of ignorance is eating and watching a scary movie, or sports, or news, etc. Eating in this mode is eating without even recognizing the food wholeheartedly, without gratitude for the food.

We can see there are different ways of eating, just as there are different types of food. As we evolve, we want to gradually raise our vibration to where we can sit and be grateful for the food.

Instead of simply eating the food, try to truly honor the food. As we learn to honor the food, more energy from the food passes into ourselves.

The main reason we eat is to get energy. In a developing country where there's a lack of food, people eat because it keeps them alive. We need to eat to live. In developed countries with an abundance of food, we eat for energy, but we also eat for taste. There are so many options. If you have the choice to eat for taste, try and remember to honor it. If you have access to abundant food, that's a beautiful thing. Let's honor the food properly so we get the full nutrients from it, and it will raise our vibration to think spiritually as well. Otherwise, if we just eat passionately or eat on the go, we'll become more aggressive with other living entities. If we eat in ignorance, we'll just overeat, and then maybe go to sleep. We want the energy of the food to transport us into the evolution of our consciousness.

As our consciousness evolves, we will become grateful for our teeth, grateful for our tongue, grateful for our digestive tract, the esophagus, the stomach, the liver and the spleen. We've been gifted, and we've been engineered with an amazing digestive system. We want the organs to remain healthy. Let's not overeat. Let's not under eat. Let's eat in moderation. There is also a time for fasting. Maybe once a week, for one day, you can try to refrain from all food and live only on water or juice. The organs will say Thank You for the break. Maybe you can try another day of the week to refrain from all violent food and eat vegetarian for one day. Then, as we evolve our eating, let's add our prayers. Gratitude for the food, for the digestive tract, for the gift of life. Eating to be alive, eating to raise our consciousness. Sit in one place, honor the food with deep appreciation and gratitude for the food and the digestive tract. This is the mode of goodness.

Mental Hygiene Technique for the Sense of Taste

Find a comfortable seated posture, either on a chair or on the floor. Spine must remain tall. Palms can be on the lap or on the knees, facing up or down. Close your eyes softly Bring the whole body into stillness. (1 min)

As you close your eyes softly, bring your focus of the mind to the breath at the entrance of the nostrils. Try not to control the breath. You're just witnessing the breath as it moves in and out. (1 min)

Now move your focus to the center of the eyebrows behind the skull. As you gaze there, imagine your amazing lips, teeth and tongue. Contemplate the water that's on the tongue, become grateful for the tongue. (1 min)

Now imagine a taste on your tongue in the last 24 hours, which was in the mode of goodness. It was fresh, it was non-violent, it was delicious, it was in the mode of goodness. (1 min)

Now, contemplate the mode of passion in the food, on the tongue in the last 24 hours, maybe you ate something spicy with chili, onion or garlic. (1 min)

Now imagine the mode of ignorance on the tongue in the last 24 hours, the taste of decomposed food or preserved food, food that was in a can on a shelf for many months. (1 min)

Now gaze into the center of the eyebrows and recognize that throughout your life you had eaten food in different modes. As we practice mental hygiene techniques, we want to start to eat more food in the mode of goodness, food that is fresh and non-violent. We can also spiritualize the food from whichever spiritual culture we come from. See yourself offering your food to your deity before you eat. As you eat, you want to be grateful for the earth that provided the food, the sun and the moon provide the energy in the food. And thank your deity for the tongue, so you can taste the food. (1 min)

For the next 24 hours, plant this phrase three times in the mind. "I will eat food in the mode of goodness, in moderation after offering it to my deity for the next 24 hours."(1 min)

Bring your focus back to the breath. Be grateful for the breath, which keeps the brain active, the tongue active, and the sense of taste active. Take a deep inhalation. Exhale slowly, bring the breath back to normal breathing. Open your eyes and go enjoy the food that's in the mode of goodness.

MIND AND THE SENSE OF SMELL

7 | The Mind and the Sense of Smell

Fragrance is all around us. We gain so much knowledge of a place, or a person, from the way they smell. What would life be without the nose and the sense of smell?

As a little fetus developing in the womb, we develop the olfactory nerves, the olfactory bulb aspect of the brain, which helps us to identify different odors.

The medium for fragrance is the element earth. The water element and the earth element are separated because you cannot smell pure water. The earth element must be present for an odor to exist. Pure water has no smell at all. Water with chlorine smells of chlorine. Beverages such as wine, beer, or juice can only be smelled because there is a drop of the earth element within them. Likewise, pure air has no odor until it is mixed with the earth element. Then we can smell the air freshener, perfume, the sewer and the garbage.

There's a wide range of smells on our planet, from pleasant and sweet, to moldy and pungent. As babies developing in the world, we develop knowledge from this wide range of different smells. Throughout all of our days, the sense of smell we become attracted to, depends on the three modes of nature.

If we're in the mode of goodness, we will be attracted to a calm fragrance such as lavender, something that is not too strong and in a mild manner. Eucalyptus is another example, or an evergreen forest, with smells that relax the mind and the nervous system. In the mode of passion, we become attracted to the sweet smelling fragrance in our perfume and cologne. The smell of a rose, citrus and spicy smells. These odors can be experienced from a distance and they raise the sense of passion within us. We might become attracted to a person because of the type of cologne or perfume they wear. It's a big business today.

You can walk into a store with expensive perfumes and colognes. All the bottles are simply water mixed with a little earth element meant to bring out the fragrance. We wear it, and we hope someone will like us because of it. There are also fragrances in the mode of ignorance - moldy smells or decaying odors. They bring the mind and the consciousness down, such as the smell of smoke from cigarettes. When we smell these, our consciousness becomes stagnant.

These smells allow us to become filled with inertia, destroying the lungs, and yet we may still become attached to it. We have many examples of humans becoming addicted to the smell of tobacco.

Sometimes a person might be in a moldy room and becomes attached to the odor, which means the mode of ignorance pervades the consciousness. Without ventilation in the air, wood starts to decay, and we become attached to the smell even though the odor generates breathing malfunctioning and lung diseases.

We live our life from day to day, hour to hour, minute to minute, governed by different odors. We get up in the morning and take a shower with a certain soap, with a certain type of the fragrance that we are attracted to. It tells us which mode of nature we are in. We may use a certain shampoo that has a certain fragrance, then we use a certain type of deodorant again with a certain fragrance. On top of all that, we put scented lotion on the body. The lotion, again, has another fragrance.

We may have essential oils that we burn in our houses. The type of oil we like comes from the mode of nature we are controlled by. You may have incense and the type of fragrance you're attracted to, whether it's lavender, rose, or cinnamon, it connects us to a certain mode.

These odors affect our mental state. Odors affect our nervous system. Odors can make us feel agitated, relaxed, or sensual. As we grow, we begin to understand, this mode of nature is controlling me more and more.

As we evolve in consciousness, we want to spend more time with odors that are in the mode of goodness. We can't avoid the modes of passion and ignorance. But we can minimize them in our life.

There's a part of the mind which is able to transcend smell. We can be in a place that has a horrible smell, but the longer we stay there, 15 seconds, 30 seconds or one minute, we may become used to it. So that means the mode of ignorance pervades our consciousness. Sometimes what initially smelled bad starts to smell good. We become attached to the odor until someone comes in and says, "Oh, this place smells horrible." Then we step outside, and when we step back in we realize the smell and wonder how we ever became accustomed to it.

As with the other senses, also with the sense of smell, when we go around, we want to be in places that raise the calmness in the mind. Take time to be in the forest. If you can't get to the forest, use some oils that you can burn with the forest nature, such as evergreen.

If you don't have a lavender garden, buy some incense or oils with lavender made from pure elements. As you burn them, the gift of relaxation comes into your mind and body through your sense of smell.

When we walk around the city, we connect to each other through the sense of smell. If you smell a fragrance, which you know is in the mode of goodness, say someone's cologne or perfume in the mode of goodness, your mind is peaceful. You give them a smile naturally.

If you're in a mode of goodness, and you find someone with a strong fragrance or perfume in the mode of passion, you may become a little jolted from it or might even feel attracted to that person.

Another time, if you are in the mode of goodness, and you smell something in the mode of ignorance, we may be triggered to walk in the opposite direction.

If you're in the mode of ignorance, and you smell something in the mode of passion, it might raise your vibration. You might think maybe I should change my clothing. Maybe I should change my cologne. Maybe I should go take a shower with this type of soap, so I can raise my vibration. Then when we are in the mode of passion with our new fragrance, we might become attracted to the mode of goodness. Conversely, sometimes in the mode of passion, when we encounter a smell in the mode of goodness, we become repelled. We might think, "I want to stay in my mode of passion." I prefer my smell, it raises my sensuality."

Another way fragrance affects us is through the aroma of food. We smell the food. We inhale and smell different spices. The smells and the food might be attractive depending on the mode we are in.

As we grow up from day to day, month to month, year to year, our sense of smell evolves. We become attracted to different environments. We feel attracted to different types of people. We even become attracted to different types of animals according to the smell they give off.

As we evolve into the spiritual self, we have something called transcendental smells. That is when someone takes a little effort to offer their incense, oils, cologne and perfume to their deity or to divinity. Thanking divinity for the gift of the nose, nasal nerves, and olfactory bulb. Thanking God for the medium of the earth element, which the odor is transferred by. Thanking divinity for this wide variety of smells that we can choose from. When we offer the incense, oils, cologne to divinity first, and use it after, it becomes a transcendental experience.

Let's be grateful for the sense of smell and the ability to dissect different odors on this amazing planet.

Mental Hygiene Technique for the Sense of Smell

Come into your comfortable, seated posture, either on the chair or on the floor. Place the palms on the lap or on the knees, palm facing up or down. Keeping the spine tall, close the eyes softly. Bring the whole body into stillness. (1 min)

Bring your focus to the breath at the entrance of the nostrils. Try not to control the breath. Just witness it moving in and out. Feeling the air moving in and out. (1 min)

Now gaze into the center of the eyebrows. As you gaze there, become aware of your amazing nose. Bring the image of your nose and the two nostrils. Become aware of the olfactory nerve. (1 min)

Explore the last 24 hours for an odor you experienced that was moldy or decayed, or maybe cigarette smoke. (1 min)

Now explore the last 24 hours, a fragrance you experienced that was very sweet. Rose or someone's perfume or cologne. (1 min)

Now, in the last 24 hours, contemplate an odor you experienced through your nose that was very calming. Maybe the lavender oil or an evergreen forest. Calm and relaxing. (1 min)

Now, in the center of the eyebrows, imagine yourself lighting an incense of your choice, or an oil of your choice. Recognize that it has been provided by divinity through Mother Earth. Offer it to God out of love, and be thankful for it. (1 min)

Mentally repeat three times, "I will try and allow myself to be in an area where the fragrances are in the mode of goodness, more and more and more."

Bring your awareness back to the breath moving in and out. Recognizing the breath is the reason why the nose works, why the brain works. The breath brings in the air with the odors. Become grateful for the breath. Take a deep inhalation. Exhale slowly, bring the breath back to normal. Open your eyes and enjoy the fragrances with your nose.

MIND AND THE SENSE OF TOUCH

8 | The Mind and the Sense of Touch

We all love a beautiful warm hug. The sense of touch allows us to understand so much of this universe, of other people, and of the environment. As the little fetus is developing in the womb, the parietal lobe of the brain is developing, which helps govern the sense of touch. As that portion of the brain, the parietal lobe is developing, our skin is also developing in the womb. Our skin, of all the organs we have, is the largest organ. There are nerve endings over the entire skin. We can connect through a sense of touch from the tip of the toe to the top of the head. Through the medium of the air element, the sense of touch has developed.

Without the air element, we wouldn't be able to feel and touch. We can't smell pure air. We can't taste pure air, we can't see pure air, but you can feel air. If you were to rub your hands, then take one of your hands and brush it over the other hand, you'll feel that air element.

The air element connects to the skin and allows us to experience touch. Once a baby is born, the baby exists in this amazing environment and gains so much knowledge through the skin and the sense of touch. We understand the three modes of nature that pervade the air as well as the skin. Whenever the mother hugs the baby, the baby experiences the mode of goodness, or we develop a sense that someone cares for us.

As the mode of goodness grows with us, we can express the mode of goodness when we appreciate someone, and care for them. We may hug a friend or a family member. This promotes the warmth of the heart. We can transfer that love from the heart to our family members and friends. We can express that beautiful space of compassion to someone through hugging. This is this mode of goodness.

When the mode of passion pervades the air through the skin, this affects the mind. We might see someone and become attracted to them physically. We want to touch their bodies, we anticipate meeting, and touching them. The first time we fall in love with someone, we anticipate our fingers touching theirs for the first time. We anticipate that feeling of passion. There is an excitement that travels through the body when someone touches us in a sensual way. We might become excited, and we can equally reciprocate that excitement through the sense of touch. We can express that throughout the whole body, through touch, in the mode of passion.

When the mode of ignorance pervades the air and the body, we become angry easily. We forget who we are. We can make a fist with our hand, and we might try to harm another living entity. Or maybe we slap someone, causing pain to them. Unfortunately, some people hit their pets too.

Some humans carve their names into the trunk of a tree. The trees feel touched too. Whenever there is touch in the mode of ignorance, we harm other living entities. We want to recognize when the modes are affecting us through the medium of touch.

As we grew up in a particular environment, we experienced different temperatures. When it is freezing cold outside, we experience cold. Cold on the fingers, nose, ears and the whole skin for that matter. This is the mode of ignorance. Then other times it's very hot, very humid. We walk for a few minutes and we're sweating all over with water coming through the pores of the whole skin. This is the mode of passion. The mode of goodness is in that middle part, a pleasant day, a day in the mid-seventies, or lower eighties, it's not too cold, not too hot.

The moderate temperature affects the mind, bringing it to the mode of goodness. The mind becomes peaceful. When it's too hot, we become agitated. When it's too cold, we don't want to go anywhere. That's why we put a heater on in the wintertime, to try and experience that pleasant temperature once again. When it's very humid and hot, we put on the AC to try and bring the temperature inside the house back to the mode of goodness. We're always searching for the mode of goodness. We might experience and like the cold for a while, but yes, let me get back to the mode of goodness.

We might experience the heat and the humidity and like it for a while. Then let me get back to the mode of goodness. Let me get back to that pleasant temperature. Through these experiences, we understand how our environment and its temperature changes affect us through the skin.

As we grow, our sense of touch develops a little bit more. We are all introduced to the element water. Oh, this is wet. Another surface like wood is dry. One surface is rough while another surface is smooth.

A pillow is soft, while a table is hard. We begin to experience the dualities of the universe through the sense of touch. We begin to understand that the sense of touch gives us so much information about what we like and what we dislike at that particular moment. It lets us know which mode of nature is pervading our mind and body.

From time to time, we might be attracted to the mode of ignorance. We've all had a fight and wanted to cause harm to another living entity. At other times, we've all been through the mode of passion, where we become excited for touching our sexual partner. Other times we care for another living entity, whether it is a cat, a dog or another person. We hug them, and we care for them in the mode of goodness. We carry these experiences in the mind, and we have memories of the sense of touch. As we reflect on memories, we might realize, we want more of a certain kind of touch.

We want to evolve as we go through our days. We want less experiences of contact that hurts another living entity, and more experiences of touch through the skin of caring for another living entity.

We keep the skin in the mode of goodness by taking a shower, using lotion, and dry brushing. The skin is in the mode of passion when we are working very hard or doing something athletic, these make the skin get sweaty. Sweating helps to detox the body from the type of food and liquids we eat and drink. The skin sweats it out. The skin enters the mode of ignorance by not taking a shower for a few days. Bacteria grows on the epidermis, and our skin starts to emit unpleasant smells.

Depending on the type of mode that we're in, we will be attracted to the skin in different modes. You might enjoy the skin being dirty, sweaty, or you like it being clean and fresh. As we evolve throughout the day, our bodies go through these three modes. Let's try and keep it as clean as possible.

If you're in a place on the planet where you can take a shower at least once a day, that's great for the skin. If possible, you can do this twice a day. Beautiful. If you're by a flowing river, you can take a dip, rinse off three times a day.

Another experience with the skin is the type of clothing we wear. As we evolve, we want to wear clothing that allows the pores to breathe fresh air. Advanced spiritual beings understand, we not only breathe the air through the nostrils, we also breathe through the pores of this skin. When we exercise, we sweat, and water comes through the pores. If water can come through the pores, air can also move through the pores. That's why when we sit still for mental hygiene going into something deeper for a spiritual journey, we want to wear loose clothing. Clothing that is made from cotton or wool allows us to breathe through the entire skin.

Let's raise our vibration. Appreciate and cherish the sense of touch. Some of our brothers and sisters can't feel their legs, they can't feel their arms. Someone may have had a stroke and they can't feel one side of their body. Take this opportunity to appreciate the whole skin, if you still have that gift, it's a beautiful gift. Raise the vibration of that gift more and more. Put in the work to keep the skin in the mode of goodness. Enjoy hugging your family members, friends, and pets. Enjoy taking a nice shower, keeping the skin clean. Enjoy living in a temperature where it's pleasant. As we bring the mode of goodness more and more into our sense of touch, our mind gets more and more peaceful.

Mental Hygiene Technique for the Sense of Touch

Come into a nice, comfortable seated posture. Use a chair or sit on the floor, but keep the spine tall. Bring the palms on the lap or palms on the knees. If they are on the knees, touch the tip of the thumbs to the tip of the index fingers.

Close the eyes softly and bring the whole body into stillness. (1 min)

Bring your mind into the present moment to your breath at the entrance of the nostrils. You're not controlling the breath; you're just witnessing it moving in and out. (1 min)

Move your focus to the center of the eyebrows. As you gaze there, imagine your largest organ, your amazing skin, which engulfs all the other systems. The skin around the forehead, nose, skin around the ears, cheeks, neck, chest, arms, back, skin around the fingers, legs and toes, become grateful for this skin. (1 min)

Keeping your awareness at the center of the eyebrows and imagine a time when with your palm or fists caused harm to another living entity. Your touch caused harm to another living entity. (1 min)

Now imagine when you use the skin to express your passion to another living entity. When you express that touch of excitement or pleasure with your partner. (1 min)

Now remember a time when you hugged a family member or friend out of deep, deep love. You cared for that family member or friend dearly. (1min)

Now I want you to remember a time when you hugged another living entity out of compassion. That person needed help. Remember when you were able to help someone (elderly or a child) cross the street by hand. Maybe you have been in a situation where you held on to someone until the ambulance came. (1 min)

Once again scan your skin around your whole body and become grateful for it. The skin holds the water, fire, air, and ether within it. (1 min)

Bring the mind back to the breath. As you feel alert, know that the breath is bringing in life force that keeps the skin vibrant. Be grateful for the breath. Take a deep inhalation. Exhale slowly. Bring the breath back to normal breathing. Move the fingers and toes slowly, blink the eyelids a few times. Open your eyes fully and cherish your skin and the sense of touch for the rest of the day.

mind AND INTELLEGENCE

9 | The Mind and the Intellect

At the same time a little fetus is developing in the mother's womb, the baby's mind and intellect are also developing. The mind and the intellect are what we call the subtle aspects of ourselves, because we cannot see the mind or the intelligence with the eyes. We cannot smell the mind or the intellect with the nose. We cannot taste either the mind, or the intellect. Neither can we touch them. That is why we call them the subtle parts of us. Still, as the baby is developing, as we are born into the world, the mind and the intellect are also developing.

The mind and the intellect are neutral elements, just like the elements of the body: earth, water, fire, air, ether. The baby's body grows into a young boy or a young girl, to the teenage years, and then to adulthood. The elements are neutral, but what we do with the elements can expand or contract the body.

If the child overeats, the body will expand and become overweight or even obese. If the child lives during a famine, where there is not enough food to go around, their body will be lean and thin. The circumstances affect the elements.

The mind and the intellect are similar, neutral elements. It's only complicated by the fact that the mind and the intellect are part of us, which we cannot perceive through the five senses, even though we know they exist. We understand that the subtle body influences the five gross elements that are both inside and outside of us. We understand that the mind is superior to the five elements (earth, water, fire, air, ether). The mind is superior to the five sense organs (eyes, ears, nose, tongue, and skin) and the five senses (sight, hearing, smelling, taste, touch).

Even more subtle than the mind is the intellect. The intellect is superior to the mind. The intellect can influence the mind. Imagine the mind existing in the middle, with the five gross senses on one side and the intellect on its other side.

The mind can be influenced by either of these, either from the five senses or from the intellect.

When the mind is being influenced by the senses, we can say that the senses are pulling the mind. Consider you are walking down the street, and you smell the aroma of coffee, or you smell the sugar candy cooking, and it pulls you to think and feel, "Oh, I want some coffee. I want to eat that kind of dessert." Or you're walking down the street, and you hear a certain melody of music, and it pulls you, and then you think, "Oh, I want to buy that music." Then you continue walking down the street, and you see a shop window, advertising items for sale, with the bright light shining on the merchandise. Your senses pull you, and you develop a desire for something, "Oh, I want this." You're walking down the street and you see someone selling mangoes. Your tongue tingles at the sight and your taste buds are activated. You think, "Oh, I want to taste that mango." The senses pull us, they move us from one part of the street to another part of the street, one part of the planet to another part of the planet. We are always being pulled by the senses.

The senses are never satisfied. If you please the senses, you might feel satisfied for a little while. But soon the senses will say, "Oh, I want more." In material life, we are pulled around by the senses and for this reason the mind is always feeling disturbed. "Oh, I have to satisfy this and that sense. I have to go serve this and that sense." We get pulled around.

On the other hand, the mind can also be influenced from the inner side, the intellect. As we grow in this world, and we understand the elements, we understand, "Wait, wait, wait. My intelligence has an ability to control my mind." With that realization, a person can control the senses, bringing them under control. Through the perception of the senses, we understand, "Oh, my intelligence grew from using the senses as well." You learn, "Oh, this is water, I'm going to sink." or, "This is solid, I'm going to stand." We all learn, "This is fire, I'm going to be burned." The intellect grows alongside the mind and the senses.

As the intellect evolves, we understand what is right, and what is wrong. When driving a car, we see the red light, and we stop, then we see the green light, and we go. We're always using the intellect with the mind and the senses.

As we grow older, we are amazed by what the intellect can achieve. When engineers create buildings, it comes out of their mind and intellect. They think of the skyline of a city or a village, and they create. Artists create beautiful paintings and sculptures from the intellect and the mind. The clothing we wear is a product of the elements, earth, water, fire, air, ether, but the creation starts in the mind with the intellect of the designer. We can see how a chef works with the elements, earth, water, fire, air, ether to make the food. A chef is creative in the mind, in how the chef uses the spices, and comes up with so many different variations. So, when the intellect controls the mind, the mind will influence the senses in moderation and great things can be manifested.

If you look around your house right now, the room you're sitting in came out of a human's mind and intellect. The engineers developed it. The space that the building occupies was there, but the building originated in someone's intellect and mind, when they designed it. Only after that did the building enter the material dimension, after they put the elements together, mixing water, sand, stone, fire with the cement. Organizing the glass, metal, steel, wood and the zinc. Now you have that room where you are right now. But a hundred years ago, the room wasn't there, only space. When we move from one building to another building, we are moving from the mind and the intellect of one spiritual being to another. When we leave one building and go into another building, we enter into another engineer's mind and intellect. As we are living in this world, we begin to understand, "Oh, there's that material intelligence. I can use it to create medicine, buildings, jet planes, boats, and submarines." It's amazing what we can create or co-create.

Intelligence can also be spiritualized. We can spiritualize the intellect when we connect to our true spiritual self. This already started when we ask the questions, what is morally right? What is morally wrong? As we evolve spiritually, we start to introspect deeply and understand, "Oh wait, I can develop this ability to recognize that I am just witnessing my mind. I am witnessing my senses and sense objects." Then we ask, "Who's the 'I' that's witnessing?" Another time, we might say, "Oh, I am eating." But who's really eating? If you put food on a dead body's tongue, even though it has the tongue, the dead body can't taste it. The dead body has eyes, but can't see. So when we're living, what part of us can taste and see? Who is the "I"?

The intelligence becomes spiritualized, understanding the "I". "Oh yes, I am a divine spiritual being." That is how I start to spiritualize my intellect. I am the one witnessing my body from baby to boyhood/girlhood to young adult and to adult.

Then we realize this body is also going to change, along with the intellect. It's getting older, with gray hair and other changes. The body was born and so it will naturally die. But I, the one witnessing this, continues. Then we might realize, I am the one keeping the elements, earth, water, fire, air, ether of the body alive. I am the one keeping the mind active. I am the one energizing the emotions. I am the one activating the intellect as well. That is how we begin to understand, I am a spiritual being and I can spiritualize my intelligence. Next, we recognize that every other body that I see, all the other humans on the planet, we are all spiritual beings. We are only watching and interacting with the physical and subtle bodies.

The physical body would not be able to interact with another body if there was not a spiritual being connected to the body. If the spiritual being leaves a body, the body would just be motionless on the floor. That is why we spiritualize the intellect.

As we spiritualize the intellect, understanding that I am this spiritual being, we can control the mind. Then the mind becomes spiritualized, and the mind spiritualizes the senses. The senses no longer pull us, because we understand, my body only needs so much to eat. We can eat in moderation. My body needs to breathe, and I can breathe efficiently. The eyes, instead of just seeing physical bodies, begin to also see a spiritual spark in everyone's heart.

As we spiritualize the senses, the senses begin to work in moderation. We have control over the senses and the spiritual being may journey in life, evolving, knowing that this world of duality has ups and downs, but we are only in this dimension temporarily. The entire material dimension is temporary. Grow with it. Evolve with it.

With this knowledge, we can recognize when the three modes of nature replace the spiritual intelligence and mind, they become influenced by them.

If the mode of goodness is in the mind and the intellect, we begin to question, who am I? Why am I here on this planet? Why did I take birth in this family? Why is my body tall or short? Questioning, who created the sun? Who created the moon? If the mode of passion pervades the mind and intellect, we will be driven just to want more and more material assets. We think that will give us happiness. I want more houses, cars, shoes, more, more, more. If the mode of ignorance pervades the mind and the intellect, we will be driven to harm ourselves and other living entities.

In society, we see a range of living beings. Some people are in prison because they harmed others. Some people are driven in life, only because they want more material assets. While others live in moderation as they use their mind and intellect to facilitate their material assets, simultaneously cultivating their spiritual search.

As they question their way of existence. "I have material assets and am able to fulfill my senses, but still, why am I not fully happy? Who am I? Who is the being that is unhappy?" As the mode of goodness pervades the mind, we can use that as a springboard to spiritualize the intellect.

When the mind and intellect go on this spiritual journey, they influence the senses and all of our actions. Instead of being pulled down the street, by the sounds, sights, smells, tastes and touch, we can walk through this whole planet as someone witnessing, controlling the mind, controlling the senses. When we do that, we will find a sense of inner pleasure. All of us have experienced a time when we were able to tap into that spiritual intellect, to use our senses in moderation, to not overindulge, and then to witness, "Oh yes, I am not the senses. I am superior to the senses. I am not the mind and emotions. I am superior to the mind and the emotions. I'm not even a material intellect. I am something very, very divine, the spiritual self." This is the spiritual intellect kicking in. We need to tap into it more and more on a regular basis.

Mental Hygiene Technique on the Mind and Intellect

Come into comfortable seated posture, either in a chair or on the floor cross-legged, palms on the lap or palms on the knees. Touch the tip off the thumbs tip of index fingers. Keeping the spine tall, close the eyes softly. Bring the whole body into stillness. (1 min)

Bring your awareness to the breath at the entrance of the nostrils. Feel the air moving in and out. Recognize you are witnessing the breath. (1 min)

Now move your awareness to your mind space, to that space behind the eyebrows, and as you gaze into your mind, recognize that space is where your mind generates thoughts. (1 min)

Thoughts come in and out, randomly throughout the day. Throughout the day, you also use a higher part of your consciousness called the intellect. Your intellect controls the type of thoughts you allow in your mind space. Your intellect directs the mind. A thought comes in the mind of food. Your intellect tells you how much to eat, so you don't overeat, and you don't under-eat. You have a thought that you're going to need to drive somewhere. Your intellect guides you to follow the red light, stop, and the green light, go. A thought comes into the mind when you're walking in the street. You smell something and your intellect guides the mind, "Oh, this is a pleasant smell. Let's relax and appreciate it." You might come in contact with an obnoxious smell, your intellect will guide you, "No, this is not good. Let's move away from this place."

Always know that the intellect is superior to the mind. Thoughts will enter the mind, the intelligence allows you to either follow the thought or to reject the thought. If a thought of something unpleasant enters the mind, your intellect and will power can guide you to say no. If a thought of something pleasant enters the mind. Your intellect and will power can help you to say, "Yes. This is something that entertains me, this positive thought." With your intellect, you know that you can witness your thoughts.

Place an apple in your mind right now. The apple is there. You've seen an apple many times. Your intellect will guide you to its size and color. Choose a red or a green apple. You can understand, the apple is in my mind. My intellect is determining whether it is a red or a green apple. Next, you can understand that I am witnessing the intellect too. I am a spiritual being. As a spiritual being I have spiritual intelligence to control the mind and senses. This spiritual intellect comes with pure love, compassion, empathy and kindness.

Whenever a negative thought comes in the mind, the spiritual being, who you are, can transform that negative thought into a positive thought with spiritual intelligence, just as you can change a red apple to a green one.

Mentally repeat, "I am different from my mind. I am different from my thoughts. I am different from my intellect. I am a spiritual being. I will spiritualize my intellect, I will spiritualize my mind, I'll act to spiritualize my senses, and I'll act through life as a spiritual being more and more." (2 mins)

Bring the awareness back to the breath at the entrance of the nostrils. Feel the air moving in and out. Take a deep inhalation, exhale slowly, bring the breath back to normal breathing. Open the eyelids and whatever you see, hear, smell, taste and touch, know that you can spiritualize them with your higher intelligence, with the wisdom that I am a spiritual being at every moment.

LIFE IN THE PRESENT moment

10 | Living in the Present Moment, A Present from God

Making the mind our best friend is a beautiful challenge. Each and every one of us loves a challenge in life. We see humans try to swim the British Channel. Some of us challenge ourselves to climb up to the different peaks of mountains around the world. In the Himalayas, we normally find two sets of humans. Those who are on a journey to test themselves and reach the peak of Mount Everest. They climb with walking sticks, a headlight and proper mountain shoes. Then there are other humans who might only look at the peak of Everest from a distance, they are content with a pilgrimage to different regions of the Himalayas without reaching any physical summit. On their pilgrimage, they find a quiet place to sit down where they can enter into prayer and meditation. They are called yogis, rishis, and monks. They don't have a desire to reach the peak of the Himalayas, although they know it's challenging, and they respect those who want to do it.

They know that a hundred times more challenging than summiting the Himalayas, is the journey involved in making their mind their best friend.

We see other examples of humans challenging their bodies and minds all the time. They challenge themselves on a bicycle, riding for 21 days around France, Spain or Italy. It's amazing what the mind and the body can do. Humans go under the ocean, dive down with one breath to a hundred meters, and then return to the surface. We call them free divers. We stretch the human mind and body beyond the normal limitations and we receive a certain pleasure from this. All these challenges take a very focused mind.

If we put that same focus, the one we know we have from the urge to summit the mountains, dive into the ocean, or run a marathon into making the mind our best friend a little bit more, we'll tap into what yogis call inner spiritual pleasure.

The mind, as you know, has the ability to project into the past. Hence we are grateful for our memory. It allows us to understand when we made mistakes, and when we did something right. When those similar situations appear in the future, we can adjust so we don't make those same mistakes again, and perform those good acts again. We need the memory so that when we leave home, we know how to return. We need to know our address. We need to know our history, who are our parents or grandparents. Memory is extremely important.

The mind also has that power to project in the future. We're grateful for this ability to project in the future, in order for us to set goals. Everyone of us sets goals. It is so nice when we can see where you are today and where we want to be tomorrow, next week, next month, or next year. By setting goals, we already start to influence the mind and body to transform. To go through a mental and body purification, goal setting is important.

The mind also has the ability to be in the present. Yes, our mind has been engineered to also be in the present. We only have to learn how to cherish the present moment more and more.

Unfortunately, most humans seldom live in the present moment. The present moment is a beautiful, wrapped gift from God. When we have a birthday and our family and friends give us a present, what do we all do? We open the present, anticipating what's inside, the mystery of what's inside the wrapped present.

But today we seldom open the gift of the present moment, and we miss the beautiful anticipation of the mystery and miracle of life in the present. It is important for us to cultivate this moment more and more. Again, the thoughts of the future bring with them emotions such as hope, excitement, fear, anxiety and thoughts of the past bring with them emotions such as happiness, sadness, regret, frustration, etc.

The present moment is also filled with emotions. The profound emotion of love exists in the present moment. In the present moment, we will also find God. God exists in the past. God exists in the future. God also exists in the present moment. At this moment, we can connect to divinity, God is right next to us supporting us out of pure unconditional love.

While we imagine the past to be fixed, and we want to set goals in the future, the present moment is open. When we live here, we tap into an uninterrupted love from God. At this moment, God's love is being expressed to us through gravity. Right now, if God didn't provide gravity, all of us would fly off this planet into space. God's love is here in the form of oxygen and nitrogen. Without that, we wouldn't be able to survive on this earth.

If we connect to our breath, we connect in the moment, we can connect to the vast power of unconditional love that exists for all of us.

We call it unconditional love because even when we make mistakes, gravity, breath, sun, moon are still there. This is unconditional love. God knows we're going to make mistakes. By uprooting the mistakes gradually, we're going to come gracefully into the present moment and experience divinity all around us.

The experience of the present moment has to be cultivated to make it into a habit. It's similar to when we were little children, some of us never loved to brush our teeth. Our parents would teach us, or even brush them for us. Then they would remind us every night, "Brush your teeth before you go to bed." But as kids, we rebelled, we didn't want to brush our teeth before we went to bed. But as we did it, and continue to do it, the practice became a habit. We now find ourselves brushing our teeth in the morning, after meals and at night, easily.

If you ask an adult today, do you enjoy brushing your teeth? Most of us will say, yes. Because we know the benefits of keeping teeth clean. We experience a certain level of happiness from having clean teeth and pure breath. So just as it took us a while to appreciate brushing our teeth, it takes a while before we can appreciate the present moment. The present moment needs cultivation. Every day when you wake up, you can try to sit for ten or fifteen minutes, just being with your breath. When your mind stays with the breath, watching the breath come in and out, the mind enters into the present moment. The more you do it, the more you will appreciate, cherish and live in the present moment.

You will also connect to divinity. You'll connect to the unconditional love that's around you. When that becomes second nature, you enter into a rhythm where every day you want to find a time to sit in the present moment.

When you finish those 10 or 15 minutes, you will take that awareness of the present off your seated cushion or chair into your daily life. Hence, when you walk through the park, you're in the park with the beautiful trees. You can feel God's love around you. The trees utilize the carbon dioxide that we exhale, turning it into oxygen. You'll feel connected to the trees, you'll feel connected to the earth. You'll see so many flowers and butterflies which otherwise you would have ignored.

When you speak to someone, speak to the person and be in the present with the person. How many times have you had a conversation with someone and you made a statement and their eyes were looking at you, but they asked you to repeat your words, saying "I'm sorry, what did you say?" Their body was right there in front of you, but their mind was somewhere else in the past or future. When you begin to make an effort to be in the present, it will help you to be in the present in your conversations. When you speak to someone, you will be there, both listening and speaking.

We can take that ability of living in the present to eating as well. How many of us eat without even recognizing the gift of the unconditional love of our digestive tract. Today, many people eat and read or watch the news of the past or the future. Or eating and having a conversation with someone. It will take a little cultivation. Here is something you can try. Find one meal a week, or one meal a day, where you shut off all electronics and just be with the food. Contemplating the love that's in the food, the person who cooked, planted, transported and served the food. Then connect that love to the love we receive from mother earth, sun, moon and God, which provided the elements that made the food, connecting you to the love that's all around.

Living in the present is a beautiful thing, because love will come into our hearts more and more. We'll be able to express that love in everything we do.

We can express the love into our careers, relationships, protection of the planet, and into falling in love with God once again. It doesn't matter which spiritual culture we come from. As we live in the present moment, our duty will manifest itself to us again and again. It will help us to find what goals we set for ourselves before we took this birth. We'll be able to live from a spiritual plane above the three modes of nature, above the emotions of the past and future.

Let's go on this journey to open the present moment. Experience the miracle and the mystery of the present moment daily. We'll be living our life at its fullest. Everyone wants to live life at its fullest. How do we do it? By living in the present moment. We will find that the present moment is a beautiful place as the mind and heart space expand into divine wisdom and love.

Mental Hygiene Technique for Living in the Present

Come into a nice, comfortable seated posture, either sitting in a chair or cross-legged on the floor. Bring the palms on the lap or onto the knees. Touch the tip of the thumbs to the tip of the index fingers. Bring the spine as tall as possible. Close the eyelids softly and bring the whole body into stillness. (1 min)

Bring your awareness into the present moment to the breath at the entrance of the nostrils. Try not to control the breath. Just witness it moving in and out. (1 min)

Now, gaze into the center of the eyebrows. As you gaze there, imagine someone has given you a beautiful present. It's your birthday and someone has given you a beautiful present. It is well wrapped with a ribbon. You can see the present and the natural instinct to open the present. See yourself opening the present slowly, and when it is open fully, you see it's a beautiful gift.

It makes you happy. Just as the gift makes you happy, living in the present makes each and every one of us happy. When we live in the present, we can be with our family members in the present. We can be with nature in the present. (2 min)

Imagine yourself walking in the park, you have your phone switched off. You're just walking in the park and being with the trees, air, birds, and butterflies. (1 min)

Visualize you having a conversation with someone, see yourself being a hundred percent invested with that moment, being connected to them. (1 min)

Imagine you are eating, with the phone and TV switched off. Just be there, really honoring the food, enjoying the gift of the food. (1 mins)

Living our life in the present makes us happy. The mind is free from tension. Mentally repeat three times: "I will live in the present moment more. I will live my life to its fullest by living in the present."

Bring your focus back to the breath. Be grateful for the breath, which helps us to live with awareness in the present. Inhale deeply, exhale slowly. Bring the breath back to normal breathing. Open the eyes and live life through the senses: eyes, ears, nose, tongue, skin, through your mind and intellect, in the present moment at its fullest.

Thank you for reading to the end of this humble offering. I hope the theories and practices of the book aid in making your mind and heart purified on a daily basis.

Keep evolving, we all can!

For further Mental Hygiene resources, visit

practicementalhygiene.com

About Charu

Charu has been a teacher of meditation and philosophy based on the ancient wisdom of the ancient Vedic Culture for the past 30 years. His teachings and trainings have taken him across the globe, but in 2019 he launched the Om Chandra Meditation Project dedicated to bringing 'Mental Hygiene' to all. With the pandemic, the program has switched to an online format in which he guides Mental Hygiene sessions every weekday for students around the world.

Made in the USA
Coppell, TX
15 December 2023

26175746R00085